South Asian Women and Employment in Britain: The Interaction of Gender and Ethnicity

South Asian Women and Employment in Britain: The Interaction of Gender and Ethnicity

Fauzia Ahmad, Tariq Modood and Stephen Lissenburgh

Policy Studies Institute

UNIVERSITY OF WESTMINSTER

PSI is a wholly owned subsidiary of the University of Westminster

ISBN 0 85374 809 8
PSI Report No. 891

Cover design by Andrew Corbett
Typeset by MapSet Ltd, Gateshead, UK
Printed by Athenaeum Press Ltd

Policy Studies Institute
For further information contact
Publications Dept, PSI, 100 Park Village East, London NW1 3SR
Tel (020) 7468 0468   Fax (020) 7468 2211   Email pubs@psi.org.uk

Contents

About the Authors

Fauzia Ahmad is a Research Fellow at the University of Bristol and was previously Lecturer at Brunel University. She has researched black social work student experiences and Muslim perceptions of media coverage of September 11. Current interests centre on British Muslim women in higher education, British socio-legal systems, representations and identities and Muslim intellectuals in the West. She has presented at numerous national and international conferences and regularly participates in national radio programmes.

Tariq Modood is Professor of Sociology, Politics and Public Policy and Director of the University of Bristol Centre for the Study of Ethnicity and Citizenship. His extensive publications include (co-author) *Ethnic Minorities in Britain: Diversity and Disadvantage* (PSI), (joint editor) *Debating Cultural Hybridity* (Zed Books) and (joint editor) *The Politics of Multiculturalism in the New Europe* (Zed Books). He was awarded an MBE for services to social sciences and ethnic relations in 2001.

Stephen Lissenburgh is Principal Research Fellow and Head of the Employment Group at the Policy Studies Institute. He joined PSI in 1994 after completing a PhD in Economics at the University of Cambridge and is very experienced in the econometric analysis of large and complex datasets. He has worked extensively on labour market programme evaluations, including Employment Training/ Employment Action, Project Work, and Training for Work, with overall responsibility for PSI's evaluations of New Deal programmes.

Acknowledgements

The authors acknowledge the generous grant given by the Nuffield Foundation that made this study possible. The project was one of a number of studies that built on the Policy Studies Institute (PSI) Fourth National Survey of Ethnic Minorities. It started at PSI, but with Tariq Modood's departure to the University of Bristol, the project was transferred there and in due course Fauzia Ahmad joined the team.

We would like to thank Bernard Casey and Jane Lakey for advice relating to quantitative analyses. We are also most grateful to Nilufar Ahmed, Tanzeem Ahmed, Shahanara Begum, Kusum Joshi, Shailja Kumar, Roshni Mehta, Bala Thakrar and Baljinder Virk for their assistance with fieldwork interviews and translations, and to Arpita Mukherjee for her participation in some initial analysis.

The core of the study consists of extensive and detailed interviews with seventy London Asian women and so without their generosity in allowing us access into their homes and lives, giving us their time and sharing their experiences with us, there would be no project. We are therefore particularly grateful to them and hope they will agree with us that the results go some way to challenging the stereotypes that they are so aware constrain their lives.

Summary

This study builds on the PSI Fourth National Survey of Ethnic Minorities and other studies that point towards diversity and polarity in the employment profiles of South Asian women in Britain, especially the different economic activity rates of Pakistani and Bangladeshi women on the one hand and Indian and African Asian women on the other. The purpose of this study was to further explore this diversity and to understand the processes and dynamics involved, especially as understood by Asian women. It similarly aims to explore the variables that act as barriers in preventing some women from achieving their aspirations. By focusing on the complexity of the lived experiences of Asian women, it seeks to move beyond statistical correlations and attempts to highlight culturally and religiously sensitive issues affecting Asian women relevant to sociology as well as policy.

The methodology was quantitative and qualitative. New fieldwork conducted in London with seventy women from a variety of age groups, employment profiles, educational, cultural and religious backgrounds allowed the researchers to explore attitudes towards education and employment and highlight issues of concern for both working and non-working Asian women. The research interviews concentrated on a range of issues from family histories, detailed personal employment and educational histories, experiences, views and attitudes towards work and study, domestic roles and family life, views on marriage, and identity. Secondary analyses of the Fourth Survey showed that while educational qualifications and fluency in English, household and personal characteristics all played a very important role, the most significant variable was found to be religion. Yet, one of the significant findings from the qualitative research was that younger Muslim women with relatively high levels of education were on the increase and finding new ways of engaging with the labour market (with its potential for religious discrimination) that were minimising religious differences between South Asian women in terms of employment participation and career advancement.

As the research proceeded, it increasingly came to focus on the key motivating factors and influences in encouraging women into higher education and professional employment. What benefits do they perceive and how does educational success and economic independence impact upon familial obligations and cultural norms and expectations, if at all? Are any particular jobs or careers favoured over others? Are we witnessing a move away from cultural traditions and religious values, or a modification of roles? Why would some women choose not to work? What tensions and barriers do South Asian women perceive with regards to higher education and employment and how do they overcome these? This report addresses many of these questions and also touches upon other related concerns such as marital and lifestyle choices and social identities, looking briefly at some of the complex ways in which education and employment choices can impact upon these issues.

In highlighting areas of significance and social change, this study questions stereotypes of South Asian women that often present a simplified dichotomy between 'educated' and 'uneducated' women, or a modernist-traditionalist research dichotomy. The authors suggest that younger South Asian women are confidently expressing their identities through at least two facilitative and dynamic frameworks: gender mediated through ethnicity and gender mediated through religion. This suggests that cultures that till recently might have been portrayed as opposed to the education of and employment of women seem to be producing growing cohorts of highly motivated young women. These cultural frameworks are dynamic and represent ongoing processes of redefinition and renegotiation of boundaries and identities. The research therefore calls for interpretative approaches that move beyond simplistic monocausal, culturalist or materialist explanations to ones that recognise fluidity and diversity within the religious and cultural frameworks that some women may choose to adopt.

This study offers new insights into the lived experiences of British South Asian women, and ends by suggesting ways in which policy makers and employers could develop more culturally sensitive equality policies. It should be of interest to those working within the fields of ethnicity, gender and employment.

PART ONE – INTRODUCTION

1. Background and Methodology

BACKGROUND TO SOUTH ASIAN WOMEN AND EMPLOYMENT IN BRITAIN

This study builds on the PSI Fourth National Survey of Ethnic Minorities and other studies that point towards great diversity and polarity in the employment profiles of South Asian women in Britain, especially the markedly different economic activity rates of Pakistani and Bangladeshi women on the one hand and Indian and African Asian women on the other (Modood et al, 1997). A number of explanations have been posited; for instance, Owen's analysis of 1991 Census data emphasises the economic and socio-demographic factors (1994), while a series of PSI studies have suggested that the lower economic activity rates of Bangladeshi and Pakistani women are partly explained by cultural or religious factors (Brown, 1984; Jones, 1993; Modood et al, 1997), namely that Muslim communities espouse gender roles that firmly locate women within the domestic sphere.

However, as Bruegel (1989) argues, cultural or religious explanations alone cannot account for the fact that Muslim women within their countries of origin, from other ethnic groups, and those with backgrounds in East Africa and India are economically active and educationally successful (though Modood et al, 1997 found that it was not as high as among non-Muslims from the same groups). It is obvious that a number of complex factors are at work in acting to influence educational and economic activity. For example, Brah and Shaw (1992) found the demands of housework and childcare, language and qualifications, family and community pressures, the length of stay in Britain and discrimination in the labour market were all relevant factors. In examining differentials in economic activity, West and Pilgrim (1995), basing their research in the West of England, also proposed that local economies and male unemployment may have a bearing on levels of labour market participation, though this was not a distinct feature of our study. More recently Holdsworth and Dale (1997) found that analysis of the 1991 Census data suggested that it was not childcare as such that took Pakistani and Bangladeshi women out of the labour market but marriage.

In terms of higher education, as the university authorities started collecting data at the beginning of the 1990s it was notable that, taken as a whole, ethnic minorities were over-represented as applicants and students, though not evenly across the sector. South Asians were particularly over-represented (Modood, 1993). Yet it was clear that some groups were under-represented, including Pakistani and Bangladeshi females, and there was some evidence of bias in admissions against most minority groups in the old universities. This did not apply to the new universities, where in fact they were favoured (Modood and Shiner, 1994). Some suggested that ethnic minority women were subjected to a 'double disadvantage' (Taylor, 1993: 433). By the end of the decade, however, all South Asian groups, male and female, had made progress, though it was confirmed that there was a bias against South Asians in the selection processes of the old universities. This did not seem to be affected by gender (Shiner and Modood, 2002). What was clear was that there was a continuing, strong drive for qualifications among most minority groups; that South Asians had reached rates of participation well in excess of government targets, and that working-class South Asians' participation rates were beyond the hopes the government had for the white working classes (Modood, 2003 forthcoming). So as far as new entrants into higher education was concerned there was a convergence among South Asian groups, and among males and females, though Indians (including African Asians) were more likely to be in the more prestigious universities and in more competitive subjects than the others.

However, there is a striking degree of polarisation between British South Asians with higher qualifications and those with few, or none, though the reasons behind this are complex. The Fourth PSI Survey in 1994 showed that South Asians as a group had the highest rates of participation in post-compulsory education for the 16–24 age group.[1] Indian and African Asian men were the most likely to possess degrees while Pakistani and Bangladeshi men were the least likely. Some other and more recent studies suggest that the participation rates for Pakistani and Bangladeshi women in higher education are on the increase (Gardner and Shukur, 1994; Modood et al, 1997; Modood, 1998 and forthcoming; Dale et al, 2002b). In comparison with Indian and African Asian women, although Pakistani and Bangladeshi women were among those possessing the least number of qualifications *overall*, Modood et al (1997) found that '... *the Bangladeshis and, especially, Pakistani women were well represented at degree level.*' This finding may have been reflective of a biased sample group, as postulated by the survey authors, but may also be due to 'migration and generation effects' (op cit). These are supported by a small yet growing number of qualitative and localised studies that point towards the high aspirations of young South Asian Muslim women and their participation in higher education and professional employment (Thornley and Siann, 1991; Basit, 1995, 1996a, 1996b, 1997; Ahmad, 2001).[2] Obviously, more

---

1   Space does not permit any further discussion of these statistics, but the interested reader is advised to consult the fourth PSI Survey (Modood et al, 1997) and Modood and Acland (1998).

2   Since this study was completed in 2001, work has begun to be published by the ESRC Project on 'The Labour Market Prospects for Bangladeshi and Pakistani Women', eg, Dale et al, 2002a and Dale et al, 2002b.

research into the reasons why such diversity exists in participation rates is required. Parental occupation and education levels, the type of school attended, the opportunities offered and the expectations and levels of encouragement for further study from teachers are 'class-related' effects which do have *some* bearing on study patterns (Modood, forthcoming).

The purpose of this study therefore was to explore further the acknowledged diversity in South Asian women's education participation rates and economic profiles by revisiting the large Fourth Survey dataset in order to identify more rigorously the variables that might account for this diversity. This study does not aim to suggest that 'all women should be in employment', but rather attempts to understand the concepts and dynamics involved in explaining women's educational and employment profiles, to discover what South Asian women themselves aspire to, and to identify what factors, in their opinions, facilitate the realisation of their aspirations. It similarly aims to explore the variables involved that act as barriers preventing women from achieving their aspirations. The study aims to focus on the complexity of the lived experiences of South Asian women and to move beyond statistical correlations in an attempt to offer policy makers culturally sensitive equal opportunities strategies and contribute towards larger sociological debates on the experiences and aspirations of British South Asian women.

METHODOLOGY

While many projects have contextualised their qualitative work within statistical findings, the study reported here took this one step further and aimed to incorporate qualitative findings into a further layer of statistical modelling. The methodology was therefore both quantitative and qualitative in order to ensure that both qualitative and quantitative aspects were closely linked and mutually informing of each other, but also with a view to producing more refined and specific models of economic activity that are particular to South Asian groups.

We began by undertaking further analyses of the Fourth Survey to identify more systematically factors that might account for the employment gap between different groups of Asian women; we explored some of these, as well as factors that the dataset could not identify, in new, major qualitative work. Finally, we went back to the Fourth Survey to see if qualitative insights could assist in new modelling.

Explaining the Employment Gap

Using a sample extracted from the Fourth Survey of 1,306 South Asian women, an initial phase of quantitative analysis was undertaken which involved building econometric models in order to isolate particular variables that were instrumental in determining South Asian women's employment profiles. The analysis involved the construction of models which explained why women were either working or not. These models were then used to quantify the relative importance of factors and to 'decompose' the employment gap between Indian and African Asian women on the one hand and Pakistani and Bangladeshi women on the other. These models identified a number of correlations relating to employment choices for South Asian women that further statistical modelling sought to modify on the basis of ethnicity. These results were compared to work by Holdsworth and Dale (1997), who have conducted multivariate investigations of ethnic differences in female labour market participation using the 1 per cent Household Sample of Anonymised Records from the 1991 Census.

Variables such as age at migration and whether the respondent was born in the UK were not found to be significant in our study, though they have been important in other studies such as Holdsworth and Dale's (1997). Decomposition analysis was used in order to attempt to explain the extreme dichotomies between the employment rates of Indians and African Asians (54 per cent) on the one hand and Pakistanis and Bangladeshis (10 per cent) on the other and the contributory factors to these findings. The results of this exercise are shown in Table 1 below.

Table 1   **Decomposing the employment gap between Indian/African Asian and Pakistani/Bangladeshi women**

Factor	Contribution to the employment gap (per cent)
Qualifications	20
Language ability (English)	12
Household characteristics	16
Other personal characteristics	2
Religion	28
Unexplained	22

Educational qualifications and fluency in English were found to play a very important role, accounting for 20 and 12 per cent of the employment gap respectively. Household and personal characteristics explained about 18 per cent of the gap, but *the most significant variable was found to be religion.* This accounted for just over a quarter (28 per cent) of the employment gap between the two groups. While being Muslim reduces the likelihood of employment for both groups, the fact that 97 per cent of Pakistanis and Bangladeshis are Muslim compared to 15 per cent of Indians and African Asians explains why this single factor makes such a large contribution to the employment gap. While this seems to confirm the importance of cultural factors, an additional factor may be that Pakistani and Bangladeshi women, as Muslims, experience higher levels of hiring discrimination than other South Asian women. This was certainly the case for some women in the qualitative study, which highlights the complexity behind statistics and reminds us to remain cautious of monocausal explanations.

Preliminary Conclusions and Implications for Qualitative Research

By making use of the wider range of variables available in the Fourth Survey as compared to other data sources, we have been able to provide a more detailed and sensitive account of the factors underpinning South Asian women's labour supply decisions than has been possible in earlier studies. We have been able, for example, to show that, once variables such as English language fluency are brought into the analysis, factors such as whether the respondent was born in the UK do not have as much importance as suggested by earlier studies (eg, Holdsworth and Dale, 1997). At the same time we have been able to confirm some of the findings produced by previous research while using research methods that make the results more robust and generalisable.

The above findings have a number of implications for the qualitative phase of the research. These, in addition to those discussed above, are briefly summarised as follows:

- to explain why South Asian women were employed full time, part time or not at all;
- to explain why South Asian women were self-employed, employees, or not employed;
- to explain why South Asian women were in higher level, intermediate, or low-level occupations;
- to explain why certain differences in household characteristics gleaned from the quantitative analysis, such as the presence of a dependent child under 5, the employment status of the spouse, and the presence of parents in the household, contribute towards a large amount of the employment gap between Indian/African Asian and Pakistani/Bangladeshi women;
- to examine why religion accounts for such a large proportion of the employment gap.

A more detailed discussion of these factors can be found in Lissenburgh, Modood and Ahmad (2003 forthcoming).

Qualitative Study – Sample and Interviews

The qualitative phase of the research consisted of 70 in-depth semi-structured interviews with South Asian women from all employment categories based in London, conducted between 1999 and 2000. Our original aim was to return to those who had participated in the Fourth PSI Survey five years previously, but tracking a lot of these respondents down proved difficult as many had since moved and were difficult to locate, or no longer wished to be part of the survey. Nevertheless, of our final sample, 28 per cent of the women interviewed had participated in the original survey. For the rest, we employed snowball techniques, using our interviewers to help us locate equivalent respondents. In any event, this has not had a significant impact on our analysis and research aims.

The characteristics of women who participated in the qualitative study reported here differed substantially from those of the Fourth Survey respondents in a number of ways. As well as being geographically concentrated in London (the home of about a third of the South Asian women interviewed for the Fourth Survey), the qualitative sample were considerably more likely than the Fourth Survey sample to be employed at the time of interview (64 per cent against 34 per cent) and to be graduates (37 per cent against 12 per cent). The qualitative sample was also younger and less likely to have children than the Fourth Survey sample.

Therefore, single women and women without children were targeted as their labour market participation is not affected by childcare issues. We also wanted to ensure that the majority of young women sampled were either born in the UK or had had the majority of their schooling and socialisation in Britain. So, our sample was deliberately biased towards young women and resulted in a disproportionate number of graduates. Over half our respondents were in full-time or part-time employment (57 per cent), working for an employer and, of these, 37 per cent were graduates. A further 7 per cent were self-employed and all these were graduates who also possessed additional postgraduate qualifications, or were studying for further qualifications. There was only one woman who was unemployed and seeking employment at the time of the interview after having recently completed a PhD. Women who were not seeking employment comprised 20 per cent of our total sample and were all born outside the UK in rural or semi-rural areas. All lived in areas with a concentrated Asian population. The sample's employment characteristics are summarised in Table 2 below.

Table 2   **Summary of employment categories of those interviewed**

Employment category	Numbers
Employed	36
Part-time	4
Unemployed	1
Self-employed	5
Students	10
Not seeking employment	14
Total	**70**

Table 3   Breakdown of samples according to religion

Employment category	Muslims	Hindus	Sikhs
Employed	14 (10)*	17 (9)*	5 (5)*
Part-time	2 (1)*	2 (1)*	–
Unemployed	–	1 (1)*	–
Self-employed	1	3 (3)*	1 (1)*
Students	8	2	–
Not seeking employment	11 (1)*	2	1 (1)
Total	**36**	**27**	**7**

Note: * Figures in brackets indicate the number of graduates in each category

The characteristics of the qualitative sample are partly the result of practical considerations but are also due to the objectives of the qualitative research (see Table 3 above). The selection processes carried out in order to construct the qualitative sample were sound, therefore, given the objectives of that element of the research. The large differences between the qualitative and Fourth Survey samples, however, make it difficult to extrapolate findings from the qualitative research that can be used to initiate further quantitative analyses. Nevertheless, there are a number of points of interest to emerge and these are developed in the analyses that follow.

For the fieldwork, respondents were ethnically or linguistically matched with interviewers who interviewed in the language of the respondent's choice. Our interviews covered a range of issues, including family histories, detailed personal employment and educational histories, experiences, views and attitudes towards work and study, domestic roles and family life, views on marriage, and identity. We also focused on influences and motivating factors, such as certain individuals or events. Also of interest were stereotypes women perceived from employers and educators and recommendations women made to encourage South Asian women in general into education or paid employment, if that was a path they wanted to follow. The interviews have therefore helped us to build a picture of South Asian women's aspirations, experiences, influences and motivations. As we have already stated, our own secondary analysis of data from the Fourth PSI Survey and other studies such as those led by Angela Dale and her team at Manchester, and work done by Avtar Brah, point towards significant complexity underlying the polarised employment rates of South Asian women. These are especially apparent when we look at Pakistani and Bangladeshi women who are exhibiting patterns of increased educational and employment participation in the professions. Since the majority of these women are Muslim, we wanted to ensure that we have Muslim women from the Indian and African Asian groups. In aiming for ethnic diversity among Muslim women, we hope to have moved beyond monocausal culturalist explanations.

While the qualitative phase of the research was not large enough to enable a meaningful statistical comparison to be carried out, our interviews, especially with women from Pakistani and Bangladeshi backgrounds from both ends of the employment spectrum, have yielded some interesting perspectives around questions of gender roles and obligations, domesticity and employment that, when viewed in context, go some way towards addressing the statistical findings. Some of these will be elaborated upon below.

In order to respect confidentiality, all respondents cited in this report have had their names changed.

PART TWO – FINDINGS FROM THE QUALITATIVE ANALYSIS

2. Education – Motivations: Why Choose to Study Beyond Age 16?

The vast majority of women, including those not seeking employment themselves, identified the prospect of financial and personal independence and increased social status as significant incentives to continue studying beyond school. Improved marriage prospects, encouragement and support from the family and positive role models were among other positive factors that were mentioned. It is important to recognise that there was a considerable degree of overlap in women's educational and employment histories. For instance, many students in our sample were also employed on a part-time basis, and, similarly, some women in employment were also engaged in part-time study. Some of these case studies are discussed in more detail in Ahmad (forthcoming, b).

EXPECTATIONS AND SUPPORT OF PARENTS

One of the most significant features of our research and the qualitative interviews, especially given our emphasis on younger women of employable ages, has been the reported supporting roles that parents have played by encouraging their daughters into pursuing higher education and/or a career. Few respondents in our sample had parents who were graduates, with most respondents coming from working-class backgrounds but expressing 'middle-class' aspirations when speaking about higher education and the pursuit of professional careers. This is a feature that is also supported by other research (Basit, 1997; Ahmad, 2001). Parental influences, then, for the most part, have acted alongside the ambitions of daughters and women in this sample, suggesting a number of shared aspirations which will be elaborated on below. As one woman said,

> I think we're all influenced by parents, the fundamental influence was that we were going to get further education, we were going to continue to get qualifications and continue in education. That was always the over-riding thing ...the fundamental nature of the encouragement was that they made it such an innate expectation to complete this course that you never even question it! Skilful on their part.

> (Humaira, Muslim, Pakistani, Solicitor, 33 years)

For many mothers or women not pursuing paid work, often in the older age groups, aspirations were often thought of in terms of their daughter's achievements. Opportunities mothers may have had to gain further qualifications, or improve their English with a view to seeking paid work themselves, were either not followed up or were given up in favour of nurturing their children and investing in their children's educational success.

A large number of women also talked about the particular role played by their *fathers as primary motivators*. Again, this feature is not restricted only to 'professional' families; that women from all religious and socio-economic backgrounds talked about the positive roles their fathers played marks a profound shift away from stereotypes about 'overbearing fathers' and signifies a call for a re-evaluation of static definitions, especially in relation to Muslim fathers. Other recent research would also suggest that the roles Muslim fathers play in motivating their daughters into higher education should not go unnoticed (Ahmad, 2001).

> My Dad certainly is very ambitious for me. He's more ambitious than I am! And he is a major force because as far as he's concerned, I can do everything, you know; I can train, or I could do CPE tomorrow and become a lawyer ...I'm being unfair to him in some sense because, yes, success is measured in money to some extent, but then he also wants me to be comfortable and happy ...I always valued and appreciated the fact that my dad was ambitious for me to do well. I think I haven't done as well as I should ...you know, his dreams were right up there ...he was an influence in my politics and my beliefs as well.
>
> (Nadira, Muslim, Bangladeshi, Senior Research Executive, 32 years)

Daughters were not *always* expected to participate in full-time employment after university, though most in this study have been encouraged to do so. Education for daughters was an 'investment', symbolising that their 'value', both within the family and to those outside it, went beyond patriarchal ideologies of women as 'homemakers'. As undergraduates and postgraduates, daughters' 'traditional' domestic roles within the home were modified to accommodate their need to study if academic success was to be attained. Research conducted by Bhachu (1991) into British Sikh women and educational achievement would suggest similar trends.

'I Want You to Become a Doctor'

The *'stereotype of children becoming doctors'* (Humaira, Muslim Pakistani, Solicitor, 33 years) was discussed by many women, regardless of cultural, religious or educational background. Women spoke of their parents' overwhelming preferences for their children to study what were regarded as the 'traditional' high-prestige, high-status vocational degrees such as medicine, law, accounting and dentistry. The following sentiment was echoed by several respondents in our sample and supports other research findings (Basit, 1995, 1996a, 1996b, 1997; Ahmad, 2001) :

> It's always been highly considered being a doctor (you know, 'my son's a doctor' kinda thing), but that's sort of been the first profession a father would boast if one of their children became one. I think there's less hype about dentistry or pharmacists or anything like that, but if one child became a doctor it would be out in the whole of the community, that such and such son is a doctor, kinda thing!

> > (Vaishaly, Hindu, Indian, Senior Lecturer, 31 years)

So, parental notions of educational success for their children preferred that they be

> ...educated in some kind of profession, ie, doctor, lawyer, other professions, business man, you know, something to that effect ...there is a greater emphasis on doctors, lawyers, bank managers for some reason, and even teachers I guess ...it seems like they've got more esteem attached to them, you know, it's really an achievement.

> > (Shahedah, Muslim, Pakistani, Legal Secretary, 35 years)

These sentiments were echoed by several respondents in our sample:

> Asian people tend to go for really high, fast jobs, like doctor, lawyer, you've done something, you become a solicitor, something like that. There's this kind of ...they're class jobs, so there's that ...

> > (Neelam, Muslim, Bangladeshi, Teacher of English as a Foreign Language, 25 years)

The professions mentioned here are those that Asian communities recognise and are familiar with; for parents who were not able to offer their daughters careers advice, the high-profile professions may have been the main careers to remain uppermost in parents' minds. This was found, regardless of parental education levels or class and is supported by other research (eg, Afshar, 1989; Brah and Shaw, 1992; Brah, 1993; Basit, 1997; Ahmad, 2001).

Gendered Encouragement

Another feature to emerge from our interviews that is sometimes associated with South Asian families is the differential level and nature of encouragement that can exist between men and women (cf. Abu Taher in the *Guardian*, 7 November 2000). There was considerable diversity and complexity in the nature and degree of this 'gendered encouragement', and the quote by the following respondent exemplifies this.

> For him [brother] it [higher education] was an obligation; to me it wasn't. So they were definitely different...we were brought up exactly the same, but the way we were treated was very different and was very apparent.
>
> (Sabia, Muslim, Indian, Primary School Teacher, 27 years)

One of the possible reasons why men, in some families, may be more actively encouraged, supported, and even pressured into higher education could lie in their perceived future 'breadwinner role', and, again, the manifestation of this expectation varied from family to family. However, very few women actually gave concrete examples from within their own families, and this issue would certainly require more research.

'Standing on My Own Two Feet'

> I always related to the logic of someone being able to earn your living and being able to stand up on your own two feet.
>
> (Humaira, Muslim, Pakistani, Solicitor, 33 years)

The vast majority of women, including those not seeking employment themselves, identified the prospect of increased social status and financial and personal independence as significant incentives to continue studying beyond school. Chief among the benefits stressed in seeking degree-level qualifications and professional careers was the importance placed on not 'depending on a man' (see below). Economic independence, or at least economic activity, was further viewed as a source of increased autonomy and social status within the household. It gave women (both working full time and working outside formal economies) an identity that was not circumscribed solely by their domestic roles and afforded them the opportunity to forge a set of relationships that were distinct from family networks. Women who were not working within formal economies but did occasional work in the shops, restaurants or factories run by family members saw the extra money they earned as pocket money. This prospect of 'financial independence' was viewed as advantageous by women from all religious and socio-economic backgrounds in our sample and was most commonly expressed by our respondents in terms of *'being able to stand on my own two feet'*.

Many younger women described the importance of gaining independence and confidence, becoming self-sufficient, and gaining control over one's life as benefits that were interlinked and were especially significant for Asian women. The following quote echoes the sentiments expressed by many women in our interviews.

You want to do an interesting job, you want to be able to support yourself …I had a very strong feeling inside me that I never wanted to be reliant upon a man, which is a strange thing to be obsessed by. I think it has a lot to do with stories that you hear about men becoming overbearing and unreasonable with women and that's just sunk deep into my subconscious so that was one of the over-riding things.

(Humaira, Muslim, Pakistani, Solicitor, 33 years)

By encouraging daughters to seek a certain degree of financial independence through education and careers, parents were able to 'rest assured' that their daughters were at least financially secure and independent, especially in the event of unforeseen circumstances, such as divorce, widowhood or continued single status. The following translated quote, offered by a respondent who had no paid work experience and few qualifications, helps to illustrate this.

In this time, yes, it is necessary to be educated. The time is very bad; you never know when the man is going to slap you [betray you]. If the woman is on her [own] two feet [independent] then it is good. If a man leaves a woman and she is not educated, where does she go? If she is educated and earning, then she is able to be independent. In present times, I feel this movement of women being educated and working is a very good thing.

(Urmila, translated, Hindu, Indian, Housewife, 30 years)

THE EFFECT OF POSITIVE ROLE MODELS

Other women working and studying within the family, such as older sisters, mothers, cousins, or aunts, who 'paved the way' – acting in some families – as 'pioneers', were frequently cited as positive role models. The level of education and employment participation of mothers also had some positive bearing in terms of expectations around higher education and the subsequent employment of daughters, but these aspirations were not restricted to working or educated mothers.

Many of our respondents spoke of the growing emergence and influence of peer groups and local and social networks where higher education and professional career development were becoming or have become, a 'trend' – a finding supported by other research (for example, Ahmad, 2001). Here, the development of a 'competitive spirit' within certain social circles has acted to encourage some women into achieving, though for some, this was also described as a form of 'social pressure' as the following quote illustrates:

…there is like a social pressure and prestige in the sense that if I had not studied long-term, they [my parents] would say 'what am I going to say to

people? You know everyone's daughter's studies and you do not study',
then that's the sort of attitude you come across.

(Priya, Hindu, African Asian, Financial Analyst, 29 years)

Generally though, the presence of a peer group and social circle that was
increasingly geared towards higher education created a supportive
atmosphere for the continued pursuit of academic success by women from
some communities, particularly for those coming from backgrounds previously
believed to restrict higher education and employment outside the home such
as the Bangladeshis. The encouragement towards the pursuit of qualifications
then, symbolises in essence, a recognition of residential 'permanency' in
Britain, that families are 'here to stay' and as such, are keen to take full
advantage of educational and employment opportunities. Although we later
go on to describe the potentially debilitating effect 'gossip' can have in small,
close communities, the presence of a growing number of academic achievers in
these same communities creates an interesting counterbalance to social norms
that would otherwise restrict women's choices to the domestic sphere. One of
the most interesting features of our research came from the Tower Hamlets
area of East London where a number of our Bangladeshi respondents were
brought up. Here, we found a marked drive for qualifications among younger
women, some of whom had entered into higher education after marriage and
having children. We discuss this ('The Tower Hamlets Phenomenon') below
and in Ahmad, Modood and Lissenburgh (2003, forthcoming).

Ethnic minority teachers were also viewed as positive role models and
were accorded particular respect if they were perceived as women who had
achieved success and professionalism without compromising their religion or
culture. There were calls from many within our sample for more teachers
from ethnic and minority backgrounds:

I think it would help if there were more ethnic minority teachers because
they would be able to understand the children a bit better. They would
know where there were coming from.

(Sangeeta, Hindu, Indian–Pakistani, Research Adviser, 23 years)

However, a concern was voiced by some that 'role models' alone, brought in to
speak to children on an occasional basis, would not provide long-term
solutions to underachievement in education as they could be interpreted as
'tokenistic'. Changes to the school curriculum that highlighted the different
migrationary histories and experiences of minorities to Britain would help to
teach children about their identities, for instance.

Improved Marriage Prospects

For some women and their families, a positive consequence of higher education and economic activity was improved marriage prospects and greater choices in issues of marriage. These choices could range from freedom to marry the partner of one's choice, articulated as 'love marriages', to the prospect of stipulating requirements and conditions in marriages that were 'arranged' (or 'assisted', the term preferred by Ahmad, 2001). The most frequently cited expectation was one in which women envisaged marrying a partner of equal, if not higher, economic status. The following quote is representative of this view:

> If she was educated ...she can sort of be a bit fussy and choosy as to who she wants to marry and doesn't have to say 'yes' to the first available person. Whereas, if the girl finished school and straight after secondary school has stayed at home, the chances are that she will be married off very quickly and she would have to marry the first person that her parents thought was fit for her. She wouldn't have the choice. Whereas, once you're educated and that, you become a bit more knowledgeable as to who you want to marry and who you don't.

> (Aswa, Muslim, Bangladeshi, Community Safety Worker, 27 years)

Some studies (eg, Wade and Souter, 1992; Khanum, 1995) have suggested that Asian women might 'use' further and higher education as a means to delay arranged marriages. There was no evidence in our sample that any respondents had resorted to this strategy, though a few women talked about friends who had attempted this. Our data instead suggest that most of our younger women in professional employment were able to reach satisfactory balances between themselves and their parents in the question of marriage. Certainly from our sample and interviews, a number of women did regard themselves as having reached 'the sell-by date' if they were not married by their mid-twenties and there was some concern expressed that higher education may result in women becoming 'too educated', and 'too old' for marriage. However, contrary to findings published by Bhopal (1998), our data do not suggest that this increase in marrying ages is axiomatic with a 'rejection' of arranged marriages on the part of educated Asian women. Nor do our data suggest that educated women are deviating from parental preferences, but rather that women are negotiating alternative approaches to marriage that remain sensitive to familial values. A degree, then, was perceived and portrayed as a form of 'insurance policy' and was also expressed as a family 'tradition' or 'ethos'. This was found, regardless of parental education levels or class and is supported by other research (eg, Afshar, 1989; Brah and Shaw, 1992; Brah, 1993; Basit, 1996a, 1996b; Ahmad, 2001).

Personal Experiences of Higher Education

Forty per cent of our respondents were graduates. Experiences of higher education were overwhelmingly positive as women ascribed a number of personal and social benefits to degree-level study. Apart from the social enjoyment of being at university, higher education was seen to bestow a number of benefits such as an increased knowledge base, increased confidence, self-esteem and self-awareness, preparing them for future employment and exposing them to other cultures. The following quote is illustrative:

> Very positive. I think it certainly broadened my horizons on lots of different levels – academically, I'd like to go back and study further. On other aspects, like socially, I've met lots of interesting people that I wouldn't have got to meet except at university where there are so many international students coming. And it's wonderful to see how so many different people can be together without things like racism and without worrying about who comes from where and financial status or anything like that. It's a world apart really.

> (Khalida, Muslim, Bangladeshi, Civil Servant, 23 years)

A few women mentioned problems, citing heavy workloads and the cumulative burdens of juggling both study and domestic commitments if they were students who were either married with young children or were working and studying part time. A small minority of students and former graduates also encountered racist sentiments while at university.

Overall, though, experiences of higher education, whether students lived at home or on campus, were viewed positively and, contrary to Bhopal (1997, 1998), were not perceived as experiences that acted to 'dislocate' women from their religions and cultures. Rather, many of our respondents, especially those with parents who expressed concern over the 'Westernising influences' of higher education, felt that their experiences had helped in rationalising their thoughts regarding their religion and culture in a positive sense.

Alternative Routes to Higher Education

Some in our sample found that alternative qualifications to traditional A levels, such as BTech, ONDs and HNDs, provided a more accessible route into degree-level study as well as providing them with a vocational element to their higher education. While some women had chosen to retake A levels in order to gain entry into a specific institution or course, others were determined to make the best use of the grades they achieved at a first A-level sitting, even if this meant modifying their initial course and institutional choices. These varying strategies highlight the value accorded to the acquisition of a degree-level qualification.

3. Employment – Attitudes Towards Paid Work

One of the areas of overwhelming agreement cutting across religious, ethnic, employment and age differences was the importance women placed on individual choice when deciding whether or not to work. The theme of 'independence' and self-sufficiency resonated throughout when women discussed paid employment. Virtually all women across religious, ethnic, employment and age divides agreed that employment and educational opportunities should be available for all women *if* they wanted to pursue these avenues. This 'if' and the importance of personal choice is the crucial point of juncture between those women who spoke about choosing to stay at home and those who chose to work.

> I think it is a very good, very positive thing. I think women have to gain control of their lives rather than depending on men. I think women needing financial security is very important.
>
> (Mumtaz, Muslim, Pakistani, Doctor, 41 years)

> I think it is a good thing because, you know, like in the old days where there only used to be like men working, I think it got to a stage where it got really biased and women were sort of at home or always dependent upon men and that situation is now dramatically reversed in the sense that women are now standing on their own two feet, making a living and in some cases maybe even doing better than men or equal to men. So I think the role is slightly changing now and I think that is something that affects pregnant mothers as well. Now I notice a lot of people in my family and also work have decided to come back to work early and it could actually be their husbands that are at home looking after their baby for two months. So it just shows a total change in the environment.
>
> (Priya, Hindu, African Asian, Financial Analyst, 29 years)

Respondents not seeking employment also voiced positive opinions about paid employment outside the domestic realm, though many prefaced their comments by stating the primacy of the domestic role.

> Well, I think women have every right to work if they choose to work. But I also feel that they shouldn't neglect their children, that they should be

there for when children have returned from school as it's crucial that a mother is there for the children and not the children who let themselves in and stay in the house all by themselves ...If the man is capable of taking care of his family and providing for their needs, then by all means I don't think a woman should go out and work unless she herself wishes to do so ...If they are not married, and they have no children, then they can work as they choose. There's no hindrance there; it's to do with choice really.

> (Hamida, translated, Muslim, African Asian, Housewife, 36 years)

Again, the importance of the male '*breadwinner role*' (see above) was stressed most often by women not seeking employment, and was a familiar concept within most social circles, though not all families were 'dictated' by this as a cultural or social norm.

Although I am working, at the end of the day if I decide to get married I would expect my husband would be able to provide for me.

> (Priya, Hindu, African Asian, Financial Analyst, 29 years)

As we can see, there was a marked *gendering of obligations* expressed by women from diverse educational, ethnic and religious backgrounds, though this was not consistent and may well become increasingly dependent upon individual opinions and experiences. Where differing roles were expressed, as in responses from Bangladeshi women for instance, favoured jobs for men were those with good financial prospects such as engineering and computing.

Employment Preferences: Good Jobs/Bad Jobs

An interesting distinction to emerge from our interviews was differences in generational perceptions of the concept of employment. Some women spoke of their parents' attitudes towards women working that encompassed the notion of a 'job' as opposed to a 'career'. For instance,

Women could have jobs but not careers ...I mean, let's have jobs, but once they got married their job would be looking after the husband, looking after the children and there would not be a career as such. But now, in my generation, a career is an option.

> (Sabia, Muslim, Indian, Primary School Teacher, 27 years)

Employment preferences largely followed study choices described earlier, with a definite preference towards high-prestige occupations. Teaching and community work were also highly regarded by most in our sample. Muslim women further identified careers on the basis of social acceptability on the grounds of religion and 'suitability'. For example,

> My dad would never allow me or be happy with me to work behind the bar because it involves working with alcohol, and, for the same reasons, I wouldn't work there.
>
> (Khalida, Muslim, Bangladeshi, Civil Servant, 23 years)

Some women, as we have already indicated, suggested that a gendered division of employment *should* exist, based on women's domestic roles, and to this were added concerns with 'female honour'. Examples of compromising professions or 'bad jobs' were those that were considered 'masculine' such as manual work (working on a construction site, lorry driver, dustman), or jobs where certain uniforms would contravene accepted norms of respectability, for example jobs with short dresses, or jobs where few or no clothes were required, such as lifeguard, modelling or stripper.

Attitudes towards men and careers were expressed along similar lines in terms of the high-prestige professions, but other lucrative careers were also included, such as engineering and computing; again it was stressed that responsibility and future financial obligations within the family meant that it was men that should pursue such jobs.

TENSIONS IN EMPLOYMENT AND STUDY

Community Pressure and Gossip – 'Success in a Prada Bag'

Jobs that involved international travel and living away from home were a source of tension for some women and their families. An example was cited by a Muslim Bangladeshi respondent regarding her cousin who was a successful architect in her late twenties who designed catwalks for fashion shows around the world. Despite her success, her parents' concern revolved around her single status while travelling around the world unchaperoned, which was also a source of local gossip. The respondent expressed some frustration with this attitude,

> I mean, she comes to weddings and looks fabulous and she's got a Prada bag and she's got really expensive shoes, but our people don't recognise things like that; *they don't see success in a Prada bag* (laughs), they think, 'oh God, she's travelling around the world'.
>
> (Nadira, Muslim, Bangladeshi, Senior Research Executive, 32 years)

This quote highlights the complexities associated with the status of 'professional', where the acquisition of certain 'success symbols' such as designer bags may not be accepted as a universal sign of success.

Another source of gossip was the question of working wives and mothers in general. For some women with young children (such as Bangladeshi women in our sample) who sought to continue with their working lives, there was a cost in terms of personal credibility and loss of 'face' in their communities, even if they chose to rely on the assistance of close relatives for childcare. For example, one respondent of Bangladeshi background described how another young woman in her local familial social circle was talked about when she attempted to continue working soon after the birth of her children whom she left in the care of her mother. According to local opinion, this woman had relied 'too much' on her own mother (who suffered from a number of ailments) for childcare while she pursued a job.

> ...I think when the baby was six weeks old she left the baby with her mum, like eight hours during the day and people talked, cos it's not fair that the mum should look after the child because she's always ill anyway, plus she had young kids herself ...people talked about her, saying she shouldn't have left the kids with the mother, it's not fair on her. And then she had another one [baby]. And she left this one at four weeks. I think if you're neglecting your family, then they do talk about you, and the daughter resented the fact that the grandmother was called 'mum' by the daughter ...but, you know, she should have stayed home to be a mother if she really wanted that. Or at least work part time or do something. You get talked about whatever you do.

> > (Aswa, Muslim, Bangladeshi, Community Safety Worker, 27 years)

Gossip has therefore emerged as a constraining feature and social regulator for many women in our sample, acting to organise, control or interfere with the aspirations and everyday lives of South Asian women sometimes in extreme and overt ways. This was especially so in closely knit communities such as the Bangladeshis in Tower Hamlets.

Juggling Study, Work and Domestic Obligations

Many women spoke of expectations and obligations of domestic and caring responsibilities, most of which are discussed in some detail under 'Barriers to Employment'. Women from all backgrounds agreed that institutions did not do enough to support women with families. For some, the pressure to continue working in order to support and contribute to family finances was a source of tension, especially if childcare was an issue.

In many cases women were happy to continue working out of choice, but expressed some resentment over the lack of support they received, both institutionally and privately, when attempting to manage the multiple responsibilities of work and home. For some women, this resulted in a considerable amount of personal sacrifice:

> If you are willing to go to the top, there are a lot of sacrifices that you will probably have to make with regards to ...you might not be able to see

your family, your children and things like that. You might be at meetings, your house might be probably suffering going to the top, so it depends on what your priorities are.

(Shailu, Hindu, African Asian, Careers Adviser, 40 years)

The pressures of juggling a demanding job and childcare existed even when women such as a self-employed interpreter and a doctor in our sample were able to pay for childcare. Working on shifts and being 'on call', with unpredictable hours, the doctor, Mumtaz, talked about the need for organised childcare that most women in our sample, with or without experience of childcare issues, agreed were important.

BARRIERS/ALTERNATIVES TO EMPLOYMENT AND STUDY

Caring Responsibilities

Both the quantitative analysis and our interview data refer to the impact of caring responsibilities for children still at school and/or looking after elderly relatives such as parents or in-laws. If we examine these responsibilities in detail, we are able to offer some explanations for these women's absence from the labour market, though we need to bear in mind that *personal choice* is another important pervading factor and is apparent in many responses. This point is also made by Hakim (1995). An opinion that was often expressed by women in our sample was the belief that the role of carer to children and/or elderly relatives was more important than the financial gains that could be accrued from formal employment.

For those women with strong views on the mothering role, juggling childcare concerns with employment would probably not be significant. Many women with young children preferred to look after their children themselves rather than leave their child with a non-family member. The reasons for this varied from a distrust of strangers to look after their children to the cost of childcare. For instance,

Interviewer: If you had someone to care for your children would you work?

Respondent: Yes I would, but only if it was a family member. My mother-in-law says that it is better not to have the money than to leave your kids with strangers. I wouldn't trust any outsiders to look after my children …I also feel it is better to go without and be stretched for money than to leave your kids.

(Urmila, translated, Hindu, Indian, Housewife, 30 years)

The experiences conveyed here would appear to support other documented empirical findings that situate childcare problems as a significant barrier to employment for the female population in general and specifically for Asian women (Brah and Shaw, 1992; West and Pilgrim, 1995). For instance, other research showed that having children below primary school ages severely restricted the chances of women seeking either part-time or full-time work (Ermisch and Wright, 1992; Macran, Joshi and Dex, 1996). Our quantitative analysis supported earlier work by Joshi (1991) which showed that once the presence of very young children had been controlled for, the likelihood of women entering into part-time employment increased as they were able to combine both childcare responsibilities with work.

For those families with elderly relatives living at home, these relatives may have been able, or willing, to take a role in assisting in childcare, but in some others this was not always possible, especially if these relatives were ill themselves and required care. Women who faced multiple caring responsibilities alongside their more general domestic duties were therefore unlikely to enter the labour market.

The Burden of Housework

A large part of the day is spent doing housework, taking them [children] to school, bringing them back; also for Muslim people they have to get an education from the Mosque. So that they have to be taken to the Mosque in the evening and picked up again. Time goes in the kitchen, cleaning the house.

(Rashida, translated, Muslim, Indian, Housewife, 41 years)

Many working mothers in our sample spoke of the limited amount of free time that was available to them, but many women not seeking employment were also constrained by the lack of spare time they were able to allocate for themselves. Why should this be the case? The Fourth Survey noted that many Bangladeshi and Pakistani families lacked various domestic electrical appliances and goods such as dishwashers and food processors. The present study did not explore this aspect any further but was able to offer some insights into why women from low-income families often spoke of having no free time or time to look for employment or study. Many housewives in our sample emphasised the preparation of fresh food on a daily basis – and, given the nature of South Asian cooking, preparation times can be fairly lengthy. The relative absence of Asian convenience pre-prepared foods may also be relevant, though for some older women this may not be viewed as an attractive alternative (see below).

Early Marriage and Early Pregnancy

Our qualitative data suggest that early marriage and the early birth of children may be key factors in delaying or preventing labour market entry and pursuing further qualifications. Although early marrying ages appear to be more common among those from the older age groups, early marriages were not uncommon for some younger women, notably Bangladeshis, who had received most of their secondary schooling in the UK. Women in our sample who were in their early forties also had young children in infant or primary schools, and their domestic and childcare responsibilities were therefore prioritised.

> Well, I got married, didn't I? And I had my children and then I came to this country. When I was in Bangladesh, my mum was still alive and, do you understand, in Bangladesh, when girls get older, their education is stopped?
>
> (Qudsia, translated, Muslim, Bangladeshi, Housewife, 26 years)

For communities with a noted low level of female economic participation, such as Bangladeshis and Pakistanis, childcare and domestic obligations were likely to begin early in adult life. There is some evidence from the interview data to suggest that younger UK-schooled women were able to negotiate entry into the labour market once their children were of school age.

A particular feature in our sample of students was the number of Bangladeshi women who were married during the course of their study. Although these women were able to continue with their studies (albeit with some disruption as a few also had young children), the completion of the degree became difficult if they married while studying. The following quote from a young Bangladeshi woman whose marriage was arranged in Bangladesh is illustrative. Although her husband was keen for her to resume her studies and she was now working part time, she said,

> I think maybe what happened was the fact that I got pregnant, and I had to give priority to that. And that's really hard to get back.
>
> (Neelam, Muslim, Bangladeshi, part time Teacher of English as a Foreign Language, 25 years)

Further research would be needed to ascertain if studying and working motherhood was becoming a significant trend.

Lack of Qualifications and Fluency in English

Fluency in English has obviously had an impact on entry into paid employment and was cited by women as a major obstacle to their entry into formalised work arenas. Some women also cited it as a source of difficulty when needing to speak to their children's teachers. Although most expressed ambitions to learn or improve their English, circumstances such as domestic responsibilities and caring for children or relatives made attendance at classes difficult. Women here appear to be caught in a cycle of barriers where time to pursue necessary qualifications is taken up by domestic responsibilities and obligations that revolve around childcare. For example,

> To tell you the truth, I have never even tried to work. I don't know English, so how would anyone employ me?

(Firdoz, translated, Muslim Pakistani, Housewife, 40 years)

Others, however, did not feel inhibited in their everyday activities by their lack of fluency in English (see below).

For some of the younger Bangladeshi women unable to speak English in our sample, attending the formal environment of a college in the UK felt daunting and, given some of the concerns expressed over the 'Westernising' influences of education, was another possible source of additional concern for their families.

Other Personal Constraints

As mentioned above, a small number of women believed that education had 'corrupting' and 'Westernising' influences. This set of opinions, if not challenged, may account for why significant numbers of young women are withdrawn from school at the earliest opportunity, and why some parents seek early marriages for their daughters. Religious and cultural concerns were cited by a minority of Muslim women, though the influence of these concerns varied. For instance, a few women expressed attitudes towards work that they believed were circumscribed by religious and cultural concerns that acted to prevent their entry into the job market. In the following quote, Nasreen, a Muslim Bangladeshi woman, also refers to the constraints exercised by significant male figures in her family though she herself did not appear to express any dis-agreement with these views:

> Women do not work after marriage, and Islam does not allow ... My relatives do not allow young girls to work. Sometimes girls find boys, this is not good you know for my religion which is Muslim. But some people like it. Some people like man and woman working, but my family does not like it. My husband, my dad, do not like it. ... Working at home [for women] is fine. Man goes out to work, man does not work inside house, only outside the house. Responsibilities are not the same.

(Nasreen, translated, Muslim Bangladeshi, Housewife, 37 years)

Here, Islam is cited as the main organising framework for gender roles, but as many other studies on women, Islam and work show, there are differing interpretations of Islam in practice that vary across cultures and social classes. Charlotte Butler (1999) notes how according to the young South Asian

Muslim women she interviewed, 'traditional customs', not Islam, were responsible for the relegation of women to the domestic environment, deterring them from pursuing qualifications and entering the labour market. Many in this sub-group, originating from rural to semi-rural backgrounds (mostly in Sylhet, Bangladesh), followed religious prescriptions they were based on conservative, lay interpretations of Islam that sought to confine and constrain women's movements.

However, religious concerns also acted to constrain the ambitions of women from other faiths from working in areas that were deemed 'unsuitable', such as a Hindu Brahmin woman in our sample, Urmila, whose family placed emphasis on the domestic role at the expense of further education or a career:

> They [parents] would not encourage their daughters to study too far because they felt a woman's first duty was in the home. No matter what, the woman would be looking after the kitchen and taking on family duties.
>
> (Urmila, Hindu, Indian, Housewife, 30 years)

She went on to talk about her own aspirations to study nursing which were blocked by her father, and cited religion as the dominating influence in her situation:

> I wanted to go into nursing and my father wasn't very happy about it. This is because of the caste we are in. Nursing is not supposed to be a very good job for a Brahmin lady.
>
> (Urmila, translated, Hindu, Indian, Housewife, 30 years)

Apart from religious and cultural concerns some women also spoke of constraints from their husbands. Concern over the potential loss of benefits, ill health and lack of work experience were also cited as contributory factors in preventing some women from seeking employment.

Domesticity as an Alternative to Paid Employment

Not all women viewed economic participation as necessary to their lives, an opinion that can be 'forgotten' when examining employment statistics (Hakim, 1995). Many housewives, regardless of religious or cultural background, expressed a positive sense of pride in their domestic accomplishments and associated any paid employment on their part as an insult to their husband's role of 'breadwinner'. In addition, the status of a 'housewife' was positively perceived by many and generally associated with the 'gentrified' classes of the sub-continent. In addition to the expressed contentment with their domestic roles many women not seeking employment felt that they were living comfortably and according to their 'needs'. So there was some equating of work with financial 'need' rather than independence:

> Well, we would have [learnt English], had we felt the need. If we felt it
> was necessary to study further, we would have tried to study further here.
> I have maintained the level of knowledge that is necessary in my lifestyle
>
> (Firdoz, translated, Muslim Pakistani, Housewife, 40 years)

In concentrating on women not seeking employment, we have tried as far as
possible to present a sympathetic reading to the voices of women in this
employment category and have attempted to avoid presenting an analysis
that suggests a 'problem' or 'victim' focus' for South Asian women who are not
working. For instance, whilst most of the older women not seeking
employment have talked about their contentment with their role within the
domestic sphere, it is important to emphasise that this applies also to the
younger women in this category and was also voiced as a positive choice by
many professional younger women. So we can see that across groups, the
domestic role is one that is valued and recognised by all women as an
inevitable part of their lives. Some of these themes are discussed in further
detail in Ahmad (2000) and Ahmad (forthcoming, b).

EMPLOYERS – SHOULD THEY BE DOING MORE?

Throughout our interviews, a number of issues were raised on the role
employers, colleges and universities could play in attracting more South Asian
women into the labour market. Opinions varied across all categories, most of
which have already been discussed in previous sections. However, most
women with employment experience spoke of racial stereotypes directed
towards themselves or Asian women in general. A number of recommendations
as a result of our interviews are listed at the end of the report, but two key
factors emerged as significant: discrimination both at the point of recruitment
and promotion, and the issue of 'fitting in'. Further discussions of case
histories can be found in Ahmed (forthcoming, b).

Discrimination

Racial and sexual discrimination was cited by a number of respondents
despite the existence of equal opportunities policies in the workplace. These
were not always found to be satisfactory in dealing with certain experiences
and were found to be difficult to implement. Furthermore, the nature of
discrimination described in our interviews was often diffuse and was not
limited to 'white organisations' but also cited by a small minority who worked
for Asian organisations. While some challenged discrimination head on, others
channelled their energies elsewhere.

Many women noted how, despite being well qualified, and in some cases,
over-qualified, they were still not being called to job interviews in comparison

with their white peers – as in the case of Senior Lecturer Vaishaly, who felt discriminated against at the point of recruitment when her less qualified white friend applied for, and was given, a post she had also applied for but was not even called for interview – or were being overlooked for promotions (see also The Runnymede Trust, 1997).

At this point it is perhaps worthwhile considering the experiences of one of our respondents, Humaira, a solicitor specialising in employment law, who herself had witnessed what she perceived to be sexual and racial discrimination in her workplace but felt unable to make a direct challenge because the manifestation of an unfair promotion of a white male colleague was carefully manipulated. She described this as 'carefully planned sexism and racism based on an 'old boy' network' which she felt was *very calculated and sinister*'. Whilst she was unable to give particulars about her grievance she did talk about how certain white men in her department used after office hours drinks in the pub to socialise with senior staff and gain familiarity with them in a way that many women, and especially Asian women, were unable to do. This point is discussed again below. From her perspective as an employment specialist, prosecution on the grounds of racism or sexism was especially difficult since:

> No-one in this modern world is going to say 'we're not promoting you because you're a woman or because you're from an ethnic minority'.

> (Humaira, Muslim Pakistani, Solicitor, 33 years)

She went on to describe the frustration she went through when deciding to pursue a grievance herself:

> I went through this massive loop in my own mind where you go through thinking, well, what do you do? Do I actually raise a grievance, do I actually lodge a claim, do I just cause a stink, or do I sit quietly and do nothing? And you actually realise ultimately that if you've lost trust and confidence in your foundation – lost faith – then the thing you do is limit the damage to your own career and make sure you don't act in an emotional way which is going to serve no purpose but to damage your career and make your position worse. That's the way I've decided it has to be. Which for any study that's being done on these issues I have to say is one of the most difficult nuts to crack, but if it could be cracked it would be superb because its not fair and not right that in order to combat this sort of behaviour you have to sacrifice your career or sacrifice your name ...it was as if there was zero integrity ...I was beginning to see why lawyers have the name, the reputation.

> (Humaira, Muslim Pakistani, Solicitor, 33 years)

Another example came from Vaishaly, mentioned above, who was a Senior Lecturer in Accountancy at a new university. She felt her contributions were not valued and her position within the department undermined when her assigned teaching at senior level courses were handed over, without explanation, to a new member of staff, a white male, whilst she was left with lower level courses to teach:

> I don't know if its racial discrimination or management stupidity, because that happens as well. Some of it is management stupidity, a few things are racial – it took me a bit longer to realise that until I wrote the points down, but having the points down – its a combination of the two kinda thing. The fact is that they gave the teaching that I really enjoyed – I was recruited as a management accountant – and I was doing that until another management accountant, a white male, was recruited and he was given that (my course) and I was left with all the bits and bobs nobody else wanted to do, which was financial accounting and I'm still doing that basic level teaching. So those things are happening; it does leave the people working here who are of ethnic origin to feel racism does exist. I just didn't want to admit that it was happening, I just wanted to deny it until these things built up, its happening, but what can you do? You can carry on fighting for it, but it doesn't mean anything to them. I've been through a lot in terms of crying my eyes out and things like that, but I don't know – its just brushing it under the carpet, that's what tends to happen, just ignore it, avoid it... The status of SL doesn't mean anything because I'm still teaching the same thing, even if I become a Principal Lecturer which is one in a trillion chance of getting that, I'll still be teaching the first years I think.

> (Vaishaly, Hindu, Indian, Senior Lecturer, 31 years)

However, such experiences of discrimination, whether direct or indirect, had not 'discouraged' women in our sample from pursuing their goals as they have to women elsewhere (Afshar, 1989).

Religious discrimination was noted by a number of Muslim respondents. Most examples cited revolved around issues of alternative uniforms and the wearing of the 'Hijab' (headscarf). This can be most explicitly seen in the following example:

> I remember going to this one job after I had started wearing the Hijab. I remember going to the interview and, before I was even interviewed there, the person made a comment about how I was dressed ...when they looked at me, the person who was there said, 'oh we're not actually looking for someone with this appearance' sort of thing.

> (Neelam, Muslim, Bangladeshi, Teacher of English as a
> Foreign Language, 25 years)

The question of dress was one that also affected non-Muslim respondents or their mothers, who were forced to abandon their Punjabi suits and saris for Western dresses and uniforms. In cases of overt and extreme religious discrimination as experienced by some of our Muslim respondents, the situation was further compounded by the absence of specific legislation outlawing religious discrimination, leaving victims open to further hostility. Other issues featured the right to observe religious rituals such as prayers, breaking the fast in Ramadan and taking religious holidays.

Working Identities

The issue of 'fitting in' with British society surfaced in discussions on whether employers should offer gendered segregation in the workplace and whether employers should do more to learn about South Asian cultures, languages and religions. There were two distinct responses to this question: those who felt that this would signal a positive way forward for multicultural Britain, and those who felt this was a step backwards and was unnecessary. Respect for cultural and religious sensitivities through the relaxation of rules about uniforms and dress codes was cited as one way employers could signal that they were 'open to difference'. However, some others in our sample, perhaps recognising the subtle ways in which racism and stereotyping sometimes manifested themselves, advocated an approach or a strategy that required them to modify or minimise outward cultural differences so that they were seen to 'fit in' with their environments. One respondent was able to articulate this particularly clearly:

> I think the more we try to fit in with them, the more we try to be like them – that is the only way of getting somewhere. Like in my role, if I, for example, did not socialise with my managers, or I decided to go in the next day covering my head, as they know it could be part of my religion, then yes, it would be regarded as, 'oh she looks different, she does not want to fit in; she does not fit in'.

> (Priya, Hindu, African Asian, Financial Analyst, 29 years)

This perspective was echoed by other women:

> I am not being horrible and that because we are in England – they [employers] shouldn't adapt to our way of life; we should adapt to theirs.

> (Mohinder, Sikh, Indian, Accounts Assistant, 22 years)

If this is indeed the case, it does not bode well for women who choose to express their religious identities through clothing practices such as the Hijab, and through other religiously or culturally circumscribed practices that challenge Western work practices such as the office party (Carter et al, 1999).

Clearly, 'fitting in' would cause serious personal dilemmas for some women. Given the findings of the Fourth Survey, that Pakistanis and Bangladeshis, especially women, were more likely to be culturally conservative and to assert their right to 'difference' (Modood et al, 1997), this issue of identity and the willingness of minorities to 'fit in' and adapt accordingly may well be a crucial feature behind the socio-economic 'success' that Indian and East African Asian Hindus and Sikhs have enjoyed relative to other South Asian groups.

Pakistani and Bangladeshi Muslims may be responding to questions of adaptation differently, acknowledging their migrant origins and that Britain is 'home', but also asserting their right to 'difference' instead. Statham (1999) argues that the relatively economically and socially deprived backgrounds experienced by many Muslims living in the UK, coupled with overt anti-Muslim sentiments in all levels of society, may go some way towards explaining why Muslims tend to assert 'difference'. Referring back to our original quantitative analysis, then, it would appear that not only do religious factors sometimes play a role in determining whether certain women enter the labour market, but also, for those that do, their relative success may be dependent upon the ability of their working environment to accommodate them.

4. Marriage, Education and Employment

Although our research focus was on South Asian women and their educational and employment choices and experiences, as we have already seen in the section on motivations for higher education study, the potential impact this has on marriage choices was frequently cited by our respondents. It is therefore worth making some, albeit very brief, comment on general attitudes towards marriage whilst also recognising the almost overwhelming tendency for many studies on South Asian women to situate the theme of 'marriage' as an over-arching and reductive feature of South Asian families – a feature this study has sought to avoid. It is also important to acknowledge that notions of 'arranged' and 'love' marriages have multiple meanings and, as such, are relational, dynamic and evolving thoughts, practices and concepts and that the aspect of attitude change in respect of marriage preferences, particularly from parents, was another clear dimension to emerge from the interviews.

Unfortunately, space, nor our remit here, permits for a more detailed discussion of these perspectives, experiences and practices yielded from our interviews, which are discussed separately elsewhere (Ahmad, forthcoming, a).

Views on Marriage and Preferences

In our sample, two women were separated from their husbands at the time of the interview (one a Bangladeshi student, the other a Pakistani employed professional); six women were divorced and, of these, four were Muslim (three Pakistanis were professionally employed, of which one had divorced twice; one was a Pakistani mature student) and two were Hindu (one East African Indian mature student, the other an Indian self-employed professional); one Hindu woman was living with her white partner, and one Sikh woman was widowed in her early thirties. This profile in itself shows a varied history of relationships that may be reflective of changing social contexts, and, given the number of divorcees (which we did not sample for), may be a reflection of patterns of marital breakdown found in white British society.

When asked about marital choices, on the whole, most women in our sample expressed fairly 'open' views with respect to attitudes towards 'arranged marriages' or 'love marriages', and there was much variety in personal preferences. Differences in opinions were to a large extent generational, with Hindu and Sikh single respondents more likely to have boyfriends than Muslim respondents. Across ethnic and religious groups, many younger women who were employed or studying stated that, while their parents expressed a definite preference for arranged marriages, they were also quite flexible in their definitions of what 'arranged marriages' represented in contemporary contexts and were not totally averse to their daughters finding their own partners.

The following quote is illustrative of this social change in the ways 'arranged marriages' are now perceived:

> I would say in terms of arranged or love marriage, I don't see – arranged marriage seems to be very different to what it used to be. You know before it was a photo or something like that of your partner, that was the guy you were going to marry or whatever. But now I think it is very different. It seems to be more of an introduction whereby you know you are introduced to a new guy and if you do not like him, then fair enough, you do not need to see each other again, whereas if you do, then great. So there is a lot more variety, a lot more leniency now, which is fine. ...I do not think that there is a problem with arranged marriages as they are called now, but really they are an arranged introduction.

(Gita, Hindu, African Asian, Dental student, 22 years)

Older women, however, who were not seeking employment, were much clearer in their stated preference for arranged marriages.

> In my view, love marriages don't last for very long, you understand. If two people fight, parents can't say anything; parents say that you got married yourselves so you sort it out. So in the end, it leads to a break-up. In an arranged marriage the parents are involved. Our parents are involved and, even when there is the slightest problem, they help to sort it out.

(Rashida, Muslim, Indian, Housewife, 41 years)

However, in contrast to Bhopal (1997), who associates high levels of education with a rejection of customs such as arranged marriages, our findings suggest a more complex approach demonstrated by the preference for, or modification of an 'arranged' (or assisted) marriage by a significant number of younger, educated women. This is discussed in more detail in Ahmad (2000) and Ahmad (forthcoming, a).

Tensions/Concerns around Education and Marriage

There were some concerns expressed by both younger women and their mothers, across religious and ethnic groups, over marriage prospects. Despite possessing a degree which, as we have discussed previously, was seen by many as necessary in securing a suitably educated husband and for securing a certain degree of financial independence, there was a concern expressed that women could become 'too educated', to the point of 'pricing themselves outside the marriage market', and 'too old'. Another popular euphemism that was often expressed was 'reaching the sell-by date'. For example,

> I am twenty-three and my mother already thinks I should be married and have a child. I think I am too young
>
> (Sangeeta, Research Advisor, Hindu, Indian-Pakistani, 23 years)

And:

> If I spent another 3 years studying on top of my 3 years it would have meant I would have passed the sort of 'sell-by date' of getting married if you see what I mean! So, [laughs], it was pressure on – if 'you're gonna study further, we'll only give you one more year', kinda thing, so straight away it was like getting married, and things like that.

> *Interviewer:* What did you understand by the 'sell-by date'?

> I'm one of the eldest in our sort of community to get married at the age of 27 and got engaged at 24. The reason for the 3 year gap was the immigration and waiting for that to get through, otherwise I would have been married at 24 anyway, but umm, that's what I mean – its pretty 'old' according to their standards, but to me I don't think I would have been ever ready to get married, umm so you know, I did kinda have that guilty conscience – you know while everyone's getting married at 21, 22, and here's me at 23 still not married kinda thing, you know, it sort of hits you [laughs] and I hated that feeling. You kinda felt worthless, the older you got kinda thing, thinking you'll be the only one …having said that, my husband is 10 months younger me, because I couldn't find anybody my age, or older, so that doesn't help matters [laughs] so that was the other thing! [laughs].

> (Vaishaly, Hindu, Indian, Senior Lecturer, 31 years)

These were concerns that were generally acknowledged across the sample but were not necessarily perceived as constraints or barriers to the pursuit of higher education or employment.

5. Lifestyles and Identities

Our interviews briefly touched on questions around lifestyles, leisure activities and identities in order to better visualise women's lives outside the formal arenas of education and employment. They also helped us to gain a sense of what 'free time' constituted and meant to a diverse group of women. As in the previous section, the discussion here is limited since our main focus in the research was on education and employment issues. However, some brief mention around women's thoughts about their identities and the way they chose to spend their free time, if any, is worth considering if only to link in with the previous section on 'Working Identities' and to highlight the significance cultural and religious identities can have on the employment choices for some women. The Fourth Survey (Modood et al, 1997) and the related *Changing Ethnic Identities* (Modood, Beishon and Virdee, 1994) provide a more comprehensive overview of these issues but also stress the context specific nature of debates around identity.

Leisure Time and Activities

Regardless of employment group, the younger women in our sample described a more active social life than older women. Many younger women talked about going out to restaurants, the cinema, pubs, and nightclubs. They usually had wider social networks and a greater variety of friends, transcending ethnic and religious boundaries. The majority of women agreed that men in their families had more freedom than they enjoyed; many younger women expressed some form of resentment over this but there was some indication that this gendered expectation within families was far more apparent in the social sphere than in the educational. Women not seeking employment appeared to be the most housebound and the least likely to have friends outside their religious and ethnic group.

Working mothers also found it difficult to spare time for socialising with friends and keeping up with housework and other domestic and familial commitments. 'Shopping' as a social activity was cited by many, though it was also cited as another household chore that took up time in daily routines.

Housework also emerged as a significant activity for most women, regardless of background. There was much variation in the levels of housework done by men in families, but they were generally reported by women in our sample to do the least amount of housework in comparison to their partners and other female family members. However, many younger women working in professional careers had managed to negotiate a sharing of domestic chores with their partners. Students living at home were able successfully to negotiate a reduction in household chores, especially when study deadlines and exams were close by.

Identities – How Would You Describe Yourself?

In this section, we asked our respondents a number of questions that spanned a variety of issues from religion, culture, languages spoken and dress. Our interviewers asked respondents to describe themselves in terms of their sense of belonging, and in relation to their religious, cultural or ethnic identities, and respondents were offered a series of attributes or prompts if needed. In the Fourth Survey one of the most significant key divisions across ethnic groups was found on the question of religion as a primary source of self description for South Asian groups and this was also found to be an important source of identification in our study. The Fourth Survey identified a link between decreased religiosity and the possession of qualifications amongst South Asian groups, especially amongst Sikhs and Hindus. Whilst our data is far too small to generalise on this aspect, we were able to discern a marked preference for the promotion of a religious based identity regardless of education level and age from our Muslim respondents. This is touched upon briefly below.

Overall, women from all employment categories and ethnic and religious groups showed an impressive degree of thought around issues of identity, most commonly professing 'hyphenated' or multiple identities. The way these were constructed offers some interesting insights into women's thoughts about and relationships with the UK, demonstrating that identities are fluid and complex and had situation-specific conceptualisations. The following translated quote from Firdoz, a Muslim Pakistani housewife, illustrates the complexity and diffuse nature the issue of identity holds for the respondent when confronted with a question that is personal, yet holds structural significance, and that encompasses ethnic, nationality and religious aspects.

> We would say Pakistani, only Pakistani. However, we are divided these days. If we have to answer according to our views, we would say British Pakistani or British Muslim. We have equal rights in both countries, Pakistan or Britain...if the form asks us for our background we would say Pakistan – that is where we have come from. If we are asked what we are these days then we would say British Pakistani

> (Firdoz, translated Muslim, Pakistani, Housewife, 40 years)

A slightly younger, professional Muslim women, also of Pakistani background, but who had spent most of her childhood in the UK, captured sentiments that other younger Muslim women made when thinking about their relationships between religion, ethnicity and nationality:

My first identity is with Islam. I see myself as Muslim. And then after that I see myself as an Asian Pakistani.

Interviewer: What about British?

That's the last thing I see myself as! [laughs]

(Shahedah, Muslim, Pakistani, Legal Secretary, 35 years)

A young Sikh respondent, Mohinder, articulated the importance of stating her faith to her identity even though she was keen to stress that religion was not a deterministic feature in her daily life:

British Sikh I would say. ...although I am not very religious, it is important to what I am. I also want people to know that I am British and I was born here.

(Mohinder, Sikh, Indian, Accounts Assistant, 22 years)

Similar sentiments were echoed by others from Sikh and Hindu backgrounds where religion was seen to be a more spiritual, personal relationship that did not necessarily influence work choices, but provided a moral framework with which to guide one's life. For example:

Religion is important in my life but it is more of a personal thing than something like you know, like I would have to go to the Mandir or anything. It is more personal.

Interviewer: Do you think that religion influences your attitudes and practices to education and work?

Well, I would say it has an affect on my life in general as opposed to specific parts of my life. In terms of my education and work, to be totally honest with you, I do not know vast amounts of my religion so I cannot say that it dictates my life. But there are certain things, morals, that kind of thing that I would definitely say are, you know, guided by religion.

(Gita, Hindu, African Asian, Dental student, 22 years)

In contrast, for Muslims, religion as a feature of one's life and as a form of social identifier, appeared to be far more significant, influencing their working choices in more profound ways. For instance, many would not entertain the idea of working in a bar, or having to wear a uniform that revealed their bodies as in the case of a young Muslim woman of Bangladeshi origin, who was not Hijab-wearing, but was teased by her work colleagues for wishing to wear leggings under her shop-floor uniform which was a short dress. Other Muslim women articulated a desire to have space within their work places to accommodate their daily prayers as the following extract between an interviewer and Humaira, a young solicitor of Pakistani origin, illustrate:

Interviewer: How important is religion to your life?

Probably the most important thing in many ways, which would be surprising if you look at me and the way I live, you wouldn't automatically think that. But part of it is philosophical, not just in terms of practice, but in terms of the philosophy behind religion and Islam... But when its actually that deep inside of your core, you can't [deny religion]. You can try and it doesn't work because you just know that it just isn't the way you really are.

Interviewer: Do you think religion influences your attitudes and practices to education and working outside the house?

No. Other than I have sometimes thought it would be great for me to [be able to] do prayers and to have a lifestyle that fits the way you live, to have somewhere private to go and do a prayer – it just doesn't cater – the Western world doesn't cater for people with different religious practices... It's like all my life I've had to stand up and be the person that's different. The person that looks different, the person that's got the odd name... And its just so like you have to spend every moment of your life already being different if you are to demand these things. And there comes a point where you think its not something I want to do in a big environment, with sort of white male boffin types, to start saying I want a prayer room. First of all the concept of a prayer room would escape them totally and you would just be so forcefully telling them that you are nothing like them that you know its not something you want to do.

(Humaira, Muslim Pakistani, Solicitor, 33 years)

As we can see from the comments offered by Humaira, her faith was an important aspect to her identity even though the absence of any visible signifiers such as Islamic dress would, at first glance, have not positioned her as 'practicing'. Given the tendency by the media, popular culture and even academia to stereotype and reduce Muslim women's identities to their clothing practices, namely the Hijab, this is an important distinction to highlight and to remain mindful of. Humaira's comments also draw attention to her intense frustration between her desire for her employers to be more accommodating to her religious sensitivities, whilst acknowledging that the very voicing of these concerns was more likely to compromise her own position and draw attention to her differences in a negative way.

As the extracts above show then, *religion and Islam were cited as a primary source of identity, particularly for younger Muslim women,* but also for older women. This would support findings from numerous other studies, including the Fourth Survey and may well be part of a wider growing social awareness of an Islamic identity that some authors attribute to the Rushdie affair and the Gulf War in the early 90's (Modood, 1990; Ahmed and Donnan, 1994; Werbner, 1994).

However, also worthy of consideration were the voices of a small number of younger Muslim women in our sample who felt less affiliated to their faith or were less practising in terms of, for example, regular prayers. Here, the avoidance of applying deterministic frameworks such as religion onto the lived experiences of women from the South Asian diaspora is especially important whilst also recognising the particularly loaded meanings defining terms such as 'Muslim woman' hold within current local and global political and social contexts.

PART THREE – LESSONS FROM THE FIELDWORK

6. Refining the Quantitative Analysis

Following insights from the qualitative research, further analyses were carried out from the Fourth Survey data. These analyses involved computing separate employment entry models for Indian/African Asian and Pakistani/Bangladeshi women who were aged 23–35 and had educational qualifications obtained in the UK.

These additional analyses were not always consistent with the main thrust of the qualitative findings. Women aged 23–35 did not have employment rates substantially different from those of the sample as a whole. In addition, the employment gap between Indians and African Asians on the one hand and Pakistanis and Bangladeshis on the other was as large for younger women as for the sample as a whole. It was also the case that educational differences between the two ethnic groupings accounted for a larger proportion of the employment gap among younger women than for the sample as a whole. This is somewhat different to the qualitative research, which suggested that younger Pakistani and Bangladeshi women, especially those with qualifications, were showing levels of employment participation that were not markedly different to those shown by Indian and African Asian women with similar characteristics.

In findings that *are* consistent with the qualitative research, women with educational qualifications obtained in the UK had higher employment rates than the sample as a whole, and the employment gap between educated Indian/African Asian women and their Pakistani/Bangladeshi equivalents was somewhat smaller than for all women. Surprisingly, however, religious differences explained a greater proportion of the ethnic employment gap for this subgroup than for the sample as a whole. In contrast, the qualitative research found that Muslim women with relatively high levels of education were finding new ways of engaging with the labour market that were minimising religious differences between South Asian women in terms of employment participation and career advancement.

The qualitative findings suggest that the new generation of Pakistani and Bangladeshi women are increasingly pursuing higher education and careers. This seems to be supported by a trend analysis of UCAS university entry data (Modood, forthcoming). With the Fourth Survey data having been collected in 1994 and there being too few graduates in their twenties to carry out separate analyses of this group, it has proved difficult to uncover this nascent development. This is perhaps a task for further surveys in the series, though some preliminary confirmation of this should be derivable from the 2001 Census. Yet the qualitative work shows that religion is potentially a shaping factor in employment choices and progression, and it may still be the case that qualification levels and religion will continue to be among the most important variables in the analysis of South Asian women's employment profiles.

7. Recommendations

During the course of our interviews we asked our respondents for their views on how and whether they felt schools, colleges and employers could further encourage South Asian women in their own communities. Their responses elicited the following summary of recommendations.

- Employers should target their recruitment campaigns in areas where there are large Asian communities. Advertising in local papers published in such areas and in Asian publications would also help.
- Universities and employers could engage in more outreach schemes in order to attract and encourage more South Asian women into the workplace. Universities and employers could enlist the help of South Asian graduates and employees to act as positive role models. Some of these proposed talks could also be conducted in minority languages in order to appeal to parents with English difficulties.
- Employers could develop better links with Asian women's organisations and community groups.
- Employers need to work harder in stressing their awareness and respect of racial, gender and religious equality issues. So, for instance, recognition and respect for time allocated during the day for prayers, or recognition of religious holidays was stressed.
- There should be promotion of a visibly diverse workforce. Presenting a poster showing a professional Hijab-wearing woman was cited as a possible example of how employers could convey acceptance of diversity in the workplace.
- Legislation should be tightened with regard to all forms of discriminatory practices.
- There should be more government-sponsored training programmes and access schemes targetted towards disadvantaged groups such as South Asian women.
- Greater emphasis is needed on providing crèche facilities to enable mothers to continue working.

As we can see from this list, much emphasis was placed on the recognition of diversity and on promoting greater awareness of opportunities to communities known to experience educational and employment disadvantages.

8. Concluding Comments – Social Changes

The data discussed in this report are indicative of a period in which significant shifts and social changes are taking place as far as South Asian women in Britain, and particularly London, and their education and employment are concerned. Although our sample was biased in favour of younger working women, our study has uncovered much diversity of opinion around a whole host of issues, including marriage and lifestyle choices and identities. Contrary to studies that present simplified dichotomies between 'educated' and 'uneducated' or 'modern' and 'traditional' women, where the former are said to be actively choosing to reject their cultural and religious backgrounds, our work suggests a more complex picture and calls for a more sensitive interpretation of statistics. This is most explicitly revealed in the apparent contradiction between the quantitative analysis and findings from the interviews. It is quite likely that in concentrating our research interviews in London we have been able to capture a newer generation of women who were not accounted for in the Fourth Survey, and have highlighted the importance of conducting small-scale, localised studies that can account for regional developments and their impact upon specific populations.

For instance, Tower Hamlets in East London, where a number of our Bangladeshi Muslim respondents live, is an interesting example of an area that exhibits rapid social change. Although our data may be reflective of a sampling bias towards young graduates and students, the pursuit of higher education in this specific area should not be ignored. This localised 'drive for qualifications' (which might be described as the 'Tower Hamlets Phenomenon') reflects the number of new employment initiatives that have sprung up in this area, such as the Tower Hamlets Graduate Forum, and more recently the employment initiative led by Baroness Uddin ('People into Management'). One respondent analysed this localised change in the following way:

> You know the fact that the women are being educated in their families is quite something because most of the communities – in the Sylheti community anyway – they've come from rural, poor rural backgrounds, who haven't had much access to education and so this is like, they're very upwardly mobile now compared to how their ancestors were.

(Nadira, Muslim, Bangladeshi, Senior Research Executive, 32 years)

Furthermore, the choices many women in our sample made were subject to a number of competing forces and dynamics that the brevity of our report has not been able to capture. Some of these competing forces manifested themselves in ways that would appear, at first glance, to be contradictory practices. An interesting example emerged from the Senior Lecturer in our sample, Vaishaly (who was a Hindu of Indian origin and aged 31 years at the time of the interview). Her desire to continue studying in higher education was at odds with her father's wish to see her employed as soon as possible after leaving school and married by her early twenties. Despite working part-time throughout most of her student years, she managed to achieve a considerable amount of academic success including a career in higher education, though was going through some difficulties at the time of the interview. However, by way of compromise with her father, she agreed, at 24, to get engaged after one meeting, to an uneducated man from a rural village in India and later married him when she was 27, once her husband's visa application had been approved. As the primary income provider in her home – and the holder of the mortgage – Vaishaly was able to enjoy a considerable amount of autonomy and was regarded by many younger women in her local community as a role model.

This example, though unusual, is but one that represents the overall complexity and sometimes difficult personal choices and struggles recounted by many women in our study. Women from all ethnic and religious groups in our sample, were modifying social and cultural norms in light of new opportunities and social contexts, as shown by examples from sections on identities and attitudes towards employment, education, marriage and domesticity. Social change was an undisputed phenomenon, but it manifested itself in different ways and was dependent upon specific psychic, religious, cultural, temporal and social contexts. Our data would also suggest that younger South Asian women are confidently expressing their identities through at least two facilitative frameworks: gender mediated through ethnicity and gender mediated through religion. These frameworks are dynamic and represent ongoing processes of redefinition and renegotiation of boundaries and identities.

APPENDIX: Further Breakdown of the Fieldwork Sample

Table 4   **Employment breakdowns according to ethnicity and religion – Muslims**

Employment category	Pakistani Muslims	Bangladeshi Muslims	Indian Muslims	African Asian Muslims
Employed	6 (5)*	7 (6)*	1 (1)*	–
Part-time employment	1 (1)*	–	–	1
Unemployed	–	–	–	–
Self-employed	1 (1)*	–	–	–
Students	1	6	1	–
Not seeking employment	2	7 (1)*	1	1

Note: * Figures in brackets indicate the number of graduates in each category

Table 5   **Employment breakdowns according to ethnicity and religion – Hindus**

Employment category	Pakistani Hindus	Bangladeshi Hindus	Indian Hindus	African Asian Hindus
Employed	2 (1)*	2 (2)*	6 (6)*	7 (1)*
Part-time employment				2 (1)*
Unemployed			1 (1)*	
Self-employed			1 (1)*	2 (2)*
Students				2
Not seeking employment			2	

Note: * Figures in brackets indicate the number of graduates in each category

Table 6   **Employment breakdowns according to ethnicity and religion –
Sikhs***

Employment category	Indian Sikhs	African Asian/Pakistani Sikhs
Employed	4 (4)*	1 (1)*
Part-time employment		
Unemployed		
Self-employed	1 (1)*	
Students		
Not seeking employment	1 (1)*	

Note: * Figures in brackets indicate the number of graduates in each category

References

Afshar, H (1989) 'Gender roles and the "moral economy of kin" among Pakistani women in West Yorkshire', *New Community*, 15: 211–25

Ahmad, F (2000) 'Muslim women in higher education: motivations and aspirations', Seminar paper presented for the Association of Muslim Researchers, Research Forum, June

Ahmad, F (2001) 'Modern traditions? British Muslim women and academic achievement', *Gender and Education*, 13(2): 137–52

Ahmad, F (forthcoming, a) 'British South Asian women and Marital Choices'

Ahmad, F (forthcoming, b) 'To Work or Not to Work? Educational and career experiences and choices of British South Asian women'

Ahmad, F and Modood, T (2000) 'South Asian women and employment; aspirations and experiences', Seminar paper presented for the South Asian Social Researchers Forum, 12 May, University of London

Ahmad, F, Modood, T and Lissenburgh, S (forthcoming) 'South Asian women and employment in Britain: diversity and social change', in Asian Migrants in European Labour Markets. F Hillmann, E Spaan, and T van Naerssen (eds) (based on paper presented at the ESF/SCSS Exploratory Workshop, 'Asian immigrants and entrepreneurs in the European Community', The Netherlands, 10–11 May 2001). London: Routledge

Ahmed, A S and Donnan, H (1994) Islam in the age of postmodernity, in A S Ahmed, and H Donnan (eds) *Islam, Globalization and Postmodernity*. London: Routledge

Basit, T N (1995) '"I want to go to college": British Muslim girls and the academic dimension of schooling', *Muslim Education Quarterly*, 12: 36–54

Basit, T N (1996a) '"Obviously I'll have an arranged marriage": Muslim marriage in the British context', *Muslim Education Quarterly*, 13: 4–19

Basit, T N (1996b) '"I'd hate to be just a housewife": career aspirations of British Muslim girls', *British Journal of Guidance and Counselling*, 24: 227–42

Basit, T N (1997) *Eastern Values, Western Milieu. Identities and aspirations of adolescent British Muslim girls,* Aldershot: Ashgate

Bhachu, P (1991) 'Ethnicity constructed and reconstructed: the role of Sikh women in cultural elaboration and educational decision-making in Britain', *Gender and Education,* 3(1): 45–60.

Bhopal, K (1997) *Gender, 'Race' and Patriarchy: a study of South Asian women,* Aldershot: Ashgate

Bhopal, K (1998) 'How gender and ethnicity intersect: the significance of education, employment and marital status', *Sociological Research Online*, 3(3): 1–16

Brah, A (1993) '"Race" and "culture" in the gendering of labour markets: South Asian young Muslim women and the labour market', *New Community*, 29: 441–58

Brah, A and Shaw, S (1992) *Working Choices: South Asian women and the labour market* Department of Employment Research Paper 91. London: HMSO

Brown, C (1984) *Black and White Britain*. London: Policy Studies Institute

Bruegel, 1 (1989) 'Sex and Race in the Labour Market', *Feminist Review*, 32 (Summer)

Butler, C (1999) 'Cultural diversity and religious conformity: dimensions of social change among second-generation Muslim women', in R Barot, H Bradley and S Fenton (eds) *Ethnicity, Gender and Social Change.* Basingstoke: Macmillan

Carter, J, Fenton, S and Modood, T (1999) *Ethnicity and Employment in Higher Education*, London: Policy Studies Institute

Dale, A, Shaheen, N, Fieldhouse, E and Kalra, V (2002a) 'Labour Market Prospects for Pakistani and Bangladeshi women'. *Work, Employment and Society*, Vol. 16, No. 1, 5–26

Dale, A, Shaheen, N, Fieldhouse, E and Kalra, V (2002b) 'Routes into Education and Employment for Young Pakistani and Bangladeshi women in the UK', *Ethnic and Racial Studies*, Vol. 25, No. 6, 942–68

Ermisch, J and Wright, R (1992) 'Differential returns to human capital in full-time and part-time employment', in N Folbre, B Bergmann, B Agarwal and M Floro (eds), *Issues in Contemporary Economics*. Basingstoke: Macmillan

Gardner, K and Shukur, A (1994) '"I'm Bengali, I'm Asian and I'm living here": The changing identity of British Bengalis', in R Ballard (ed.) *Desh Pardesh, The South Asian Presence in Britain*, London: Hurst & Co

Hakim, C (1995) 'Labour market and employment stability: is there a continuing sex differential in labour market behaviour?', Working Paper 1, London: London School of Economics and Political Science, Deptartment of Sociology

Holdsworth, C and Dale, A (1997) 'Ethnic differences in women's employment', *Work, Employment and Society*, 11: 435–57

Jones, T (1993) *Britain's Ethnic Minorities*. London: Policy Studies Institute

Joshi, H (1991) 'Sex and motherhood as handicaps in the labour market', in D Groves and M Maclean (eds) *Women's Issues in Social Policy*. London: Routledge

Khanum, S (1995) 'Education and the Muslim Girl', in M Blair, J Holland and S Sheldon (eds) *Identity and Diversity: Gender and the Experience of Education,* Clevedon: Multilingual Matters Ltd

Lissenburgh, S, Modood, T and Ahmad, F (forthcoming) *South Asian Women and Employment: quantitative analysis of the Fourth National Survey of Ethnic Minorities*, PSI Research Discussion Series. London: Policy Studies Institute

Macran, S, Joshi, H and Dex, S (1996) 'Employment after childbearing: a survival analysis', *Work, Employment and Society*, 10: 273–96

Modood, T (1990) 'British Asian Muslims and the Rushdie Affair', *The Political Quarterly*, 61:2, 143–160 and also in J Donald, and A Rattansi (eds) *'Race', Culture and Difference,* London: Sage

Modood, T (1993) 'The Number of Ethic Minority Students in British Higher Education: Some grounds for optimism', *Oxford Review of Education,* Vol. 19, No. 2, 167–82

Modood, T (1998) 'Ethnic Minorities' Drive for Qualifications,' in T Modood and T Acland (Eds), *Race and Higher Education: Experiences, Challenges and Policy Implications*. London: Policy Studies Institute

Modood, T. (2003 forthcoming) 'Ethnic Differences in Educational Performance', in D. Mason (ed.) *Explaining Ethnic Differences*. Bristol: The Policy Press

Modood, T and Acland, T (eds) (1998) *Race and Higher Education*, London: Policy Studies Institute

Modood, T, Beishon, S and Virdee, S (1994) *Changing Ethnic Identities*. London: Policy Studies Institute

Modood, T, Berthoud, R, Lakey, J, Nazroo, J, Smith, P, Virdee, S, Beishon, S (1997) *Ethnic Minorities in Britain – diversity and disadvantage*. London: Policy Studies Institute

Modood, T and Shiner, M (1994) *Ethnic Minorities and Higher Education – why are there differential rates of entry?* London: Policy Studies Institute

Owen, D (1994). *Ethnic Minority Women and the Labour Market*. Manchester: Equal Opportunities Commission

Runnymede Trust (1997) *Islamophobia: a challenge for us all*, London: Runnymede Trust

Shiner, M and Modood, T (2002) 'Help or Hindrance? Higher Education and the route to Ethnic Equality', *British Journal of Sociology of Education*, 23 (2), June, 209–32

Singh, R (1990) 'Ethnic minority experience in higher education', *Higher Education Quarterly*, 44: 344–59

Statham, P (1999) 'Political mobilisation by minorities in Britain: negative feedback of "race relations"'? *Journal of Ethnic and Migration Studies,* **25**(4): 597

Taher, A (2000) 'Stuff of dreams', *Guardian,* 7 November

Taylor, P (1993) 'Minority ethnic groups and gender in access to higher education', *New Community*, 19: 425–40

Thornley, E P and Siann, G (1991) 'The Career Aspirations of South Asian Girls in Glasgow', *Gender and Education*, 3(3): 237–48

Wade, B and Souter, P (1992) *Continuing to Think, The British Asian Girl,* Clevedon: Multilingual Matters Ltd

Werbner, P (1994) 'Diaspora and millennium: British Pakistani global–local fabulations of the Gulf War', in A Ahmed and H Donnan (eds) *Islam, Globalization and Postmodernity.* London: Routledge

West, J and Pilgrim, S (1995) 'South Asian women in employment: the impact of migration, ethnic origin and the local economy', *New Community,* 21: 357–78

Other PSI Fourth National Survey of Ethnic Minorities Publications

Key Book
Ethnic Minorities in Britain: Diversity and Disadvantage – Fourth National Survey of Ethnic Minorities
Tariq Modood, Richard Berthoud, Jane Lakey, James Nazroo, Patten Smith, Satnam Virdee and Sharon Beishon
ISBN: 0-85374-670-2 (1997)

Ethnicity, Class and Health: Fourth National Survey of Ethnic Minorities
James Nazroo
ISBN: 0-85374-762-X (2001)

Ethnic Minority Families
Tariq Modood, Sharon Beishon, and Satnam Virdee
ISBN: 0-85374-746-6 (1998)

Ethnicity and Mental Health: Fourth National Survey of Ethnic Minorities
James Nazroo
ISBN: 0-85374-718-0 (1997)

The Health of Britain's Ethnic Minorities: Fourth National Survey of Ethnic Minorities
James Nazroo
ISBN: 0-85374-709-1 (1997)

Asian Self-Employment: The Interaction of Culture and Economics
Hilary Metcalf, Tariq Modood and Satnam Virdee
ISBN: 0-85374-698-2 (1996)

Racial Violence and Harassment
Satnam Virdee
ISBN: 0-85374-647-8 (1995)

Changing Ethnic Identities
Tariq Modood, Sharon Beishon and Satnam Virdee
ISBN: 0-85374-646-X (1994) (available for free, online at www.psi.org.uk)

Publications of Related Interest

Why do Black Women Organise? A comparative analysis of black women's voluntary sector organisations in Britain and their relationship to the state
Sonia Davis and Veronica Cooke
ISBN: 0-85374-8000-4 (2002)

Black and Minority Ethnic Voluntary and Community Organisations: Their role and future development in England and Wales
Mike McLeod, David Owen and Chris Kharmis
ISBN: 0-85374-779-2 (2001)

Ethnicity and Employment in Higher Education
John Carter, Steve Fenton and Tariq Modood
ISBN: 0-85374-764-4 (1999)

Overcrowding among Bangladeshi Households in Tower Hamlets
Elaine Kempson
ISBN: 0-85374-748-2 (1998)

Race and Higher Education
Tariq Modood and Tony Acland
ISBN: 0-85374-717-2 (1998)

Church, State and Religious Minorities
Tariq Modood
ISBN: 0-85374-724-5 (1997)

Britain's Ethnic Minorities
Trevor Jones
ISBN: 0-85374-684-2 (1996)

Credit Use and Ethnic Minorities
Alicia Herbert and Elaine Kempson
ISBN: 0-85374-695-8 (1996)

Nursing in a Multi-Ethnic NHS
Sharon Beishon, Satnam Virdee and Ann Hagel
ISBN: 0-85374-662-1 (1995)

Ethnic Minorities and Higher Education: Why Are There Differential Rates of Entry?
Tariq Modood and Michael Shiner
ISBN: 0-85374-633-8 (1994)